Bad, Bad BOBO

Based on True Events

AuthorHouse™
1663 Liberty Drive
Bloomington, IN 47403
www.authorhouse.com
Phone: 1 (800) 839-8640

Published by AuthorHouse 12/11/2017

ISBN: 978-1-5462-2084-8 (sc)
ISBN: 978-1-5462-2085-5 (e)

Print information available on the last page.

This book is printed on acid-free paper.

authorHOUSE®

Bad, Bad BOBO

Based on True Events

Written and Illustrated by

KALYNNE CHAPMAN

Bobo the boxer is as cute as can be, but caring for a dog is a big responsibility.

Attention is needed at all times, and this book will show you why with a few little rhymes.

As Kakes sits and eats her breakfast, Bobo stares and begs for scraps. She looks away for a second then she hears a loud CRACK!

Bobo has eaten a spoon! How did he get it? What should she do? Oh gosh! Oh no! But all she can say is, "Bad, bad Bobo."

It's time for a nap for the cute, new pup,
and it's time for Kakes to get all cleaned up.

She hops in the shower, throwing her clothes on the floor, as she thinks to herself, "Oh he won't come through the door."

She peeks out of the shower, only to see,
some missing clothes and a sneaky puppy.

She chases and runs and leaps and follows, but it's no use. The undies are gone in one, solid swallow.

Oh gosh! Oh no! But all she can say is, "Bad, bad bobo."

They sit outside feeling the grass under their feet, when Kakes sees Bobo eyeing the Pizza Place down the street!

She thinks to herself, "Oh please don't smell the pizza! Why didn't I put him on a leash?" Then soon enough, he's running toward the mozzarella cheese. She yells after him, "Stop! Don't go!"

But while scarfing down the pizza, he doesn't even hear her say bad, bad Bobo.

As they get settled for the night all snuggled and close, Bobo looks at her and kisses her nose. She says to herself, "My puppy isn't always bad, and I do love him so!" She then kisses his cheeks and whispers, "You're my sweet, sweet Bobo."

Printed in the United States
By Bookmasters